Thanks to the creative team:

Senior Editor: Alice Peebles

Designer: Lauren Woods and collaborate agency

Original edition copyright 2015 by Hungry Tomato Ltd.

Copyright © 2016 by Lerner Publishing Group, Inc.

Hungry Tomato™ is a trademark of Lerner Publishing Group, Inc.

All rights reserved. International copyright secured. No part of this book may be reproduced, stored in a retrieval system, or transmitted in any form or by any means—electronic, mechanical, photocopying, recording, or otherwise— without the prior written permission of Lerner Publishing Group, Inc., except for the inclusion of brief quotations in an acknowledged review.

Hungry Tomato™
A division of Lerner Publishing Group, Inc.
241 First Avenue North
Minneapolis, MN 55401 USA

For reading levels and more information, look up this title at www.lernerbooks.com.

Main body text set in Century Gothic.

Typeface provided by Monotype Typography.

Library of Congress Cataloging-in-Publication Data

The Cataloging-in-Publication Data for *Stickmen's Guide to Aircraft* is on file at the Library of Congress.

ISBN 978-1-4677-9359-9 (lib. bdg.)
ISBN 978-1-4677-9591-3 (pbk.)
ISBN 978-1-4677-9592-0 (EB pdf)

Manufactured in the United States of America

1 – VP – 12/31/15

STICKMEN'S GUIDE TO AIRCRAFT

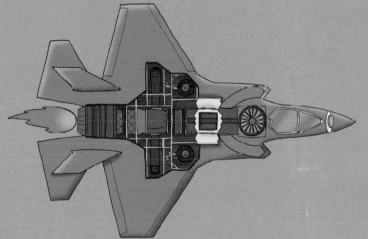

by John Farndon

Illustrated by John Paul de Quay

HUNGRY TOMATO

Powell River Public Library

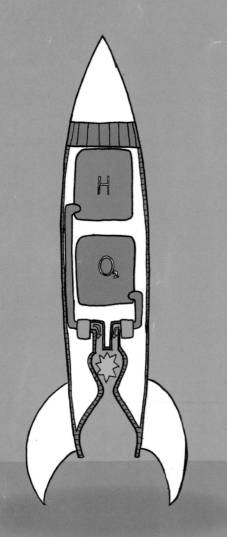

The Chinese made an early helicopter in about 400 BCE—it was a bamboo toy.

Contents

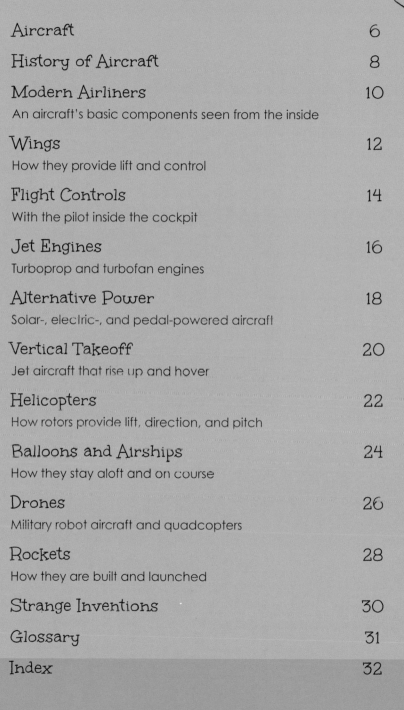

Aircraft

Air travel is now an everyday experience, just like jumping on a train or riding in a car. Yet for most people, the moment when a plane takes off and carries you into the air is still awe-inspiring. In this book, we'll explore the magic of just how aircraft work—how wings provide lift, how the pilot controls a plane in the air, how some planes can fly faster than sound, and much more. But before we take off, let's take a look at their place in today's world.

Flight Control

The air traffic controllers' task is to prevent all of the many flights from bumping into each other. They keep a constant watch from the ground on radar and send a continual stream of instructions to pilots. It's an enormous task because there are thousands of flights, and they are all moving very fast. It is thought that at any one moment there are more than 11,000 airliners in flight around the world.

A Day in the Air

On one typical July day in 2014, air traffic controllers counted almost 30,000 airliner flights over Europe alone. Those airliners flew a total of over 25 million nautical miles on that single day, the equivalent of 998 times around the earth or 104 trips to the moon.

Frequent Fliers

Americans are the world's most frequent fliers. On average every American gets on a plane two or three times a year. That might not sound like much, but it means that 757 million flights are made by Americans each year. Imagine virtually the entire population of Chicago getting on a plane every day and you'll get the idea. Around the world, there are more than three billion airline passengers each year.

How Many Aircraft?

There are lots of aircraft in the world today. Altogether there may be half a million aircraft around the world, of which nearly two-thirds operate in the USA. About 100,000 of these are military planes, and there are about 20,000 airliners and 50,000 helicopters. Some experts think there will be nearly 40,000 passenger and cargo planes by 2032.

Who Needs a Lift?

Helicopters can land on the tiniest helipads on top of the tallest buildings. The highest is a scary 1,439 ft (438.6 m) up on top of the Guangzhou International Finance Center tower in China. But Seoul (right) in South Korea is helipad city, with 12 helipads on towers over 650 ft (195 m) tall.

History of Aircraft

Long ago, people thought the only way to fly was to strap on wings and try flapping like a bird. Needless to say, the consequences were often unfortunate! In the end, the first successful flights were made in balloons. The breakthrough for winged aircraft came when Sir George Cayley (*see right*) discovered the special curve that turns a rigid wing into an airfoil that provides "lift."

1853

Sir George Cayley built a full-sized glider to make the first crewed airplane flight ever. His butler was the pilot.

1783

In Paris, a French teacher, Jean-François Pilâtre de Rozier, and the Marquis d'Arlandes became the first people to take off and fly successfully, in the Montgolfier brothers' hot-air balloon.

1775   1800   1825   1850

About 850 CE

Inventor Abbas ibn Firnas of Cordoba in Spain strapped on artificial wings, jumped off a cliff, and flew for ten minutes. Landing was harder…

1848

John Stringfellow and William Henson's model aircraft made the first powered flight ever. It flew 30 ft (9 m), powered by… a steam engine.

1852

Henry Giffard made the first powered, steerable aircraft—a steam-powered airship filled with highly inflammable hydrogen. Scary!

1782

The French Montgolfier brothers sent up the first successful hot-air balloon. The passengers were a sheep, a duck, and a chicken.

1896

After a long series of successful hang-glider flights, German flying pioneer Otto Lilienthal took one flight too many. He crashed and died.

1947

American pilot Chuck Yeager flew faster than sound for the first time in the Bell X-1 experimental plane. And everybody heard about it…

1926

American rocket pioneer Robert H. Goddard sent up the first free flight of a liquid-fueled rocket. It climbed three times its own height of 10 ft (3 m).

ROBERT H. GODDARD
U.S. AIR MAIL 8c

1927

USA·13c

50th Anniversary Solo Transatlantic Flight

Charles A. Lindbergh completed the first solo, nonstop trans-Atlantic flight. It took him 33½ hours.

1875 — 1900 — 1925 — 1950

1909

French aviator Louis Blériot made the first airplane crossing of the English Channel. He got lost on the way.

1930

British engineer Frank Whittle invented the jet engine. But he couldn't afford to patent it.

1903

Orville and Wilbur Wright made the first powered, controlled aircraft flight in their *Flyer* at Kitty Hawk, North Carolina…and landed safely.

Modern Airliners

Airliners—planes that carry passengers—are complicated machines. Yet, like most aircraft, they have just three main parts: fuselage, wings, and engines. The fuselage is the long tube where the pilot, passengers, and luggage are carried. Two big wings on either side lift the aircraft, and two little wings and a fin at the rear provide control. The engines power the aircraft through the air.

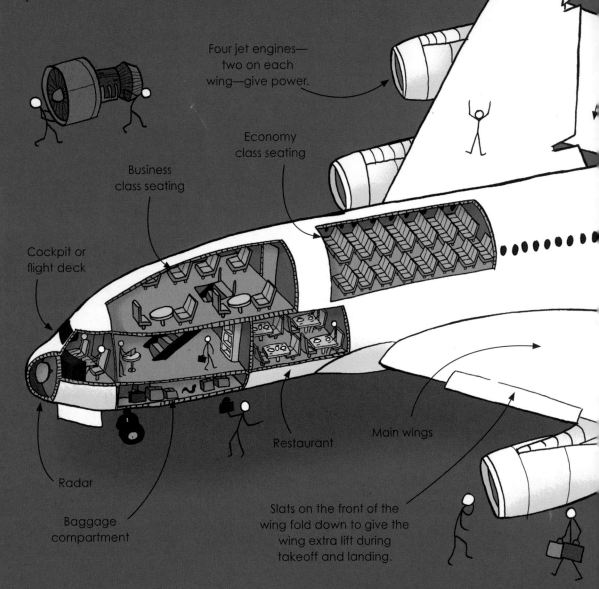

Four jet engines—two on each wing—give power.

Economy class seating

Business class seating

Cockpit or flight deck

Radar

Baggage compartment

Restaurant

Main wings

Slats on the front of the wing fold down to give the wing extra lift during takeoff and landing.

Inside an Airliner

This is the world's largest airliner, the Airbus A380. It has two decks and can carry up to 853 people at a time. It's so big that some versions have bars and restaurants for passengers to use on long flights.

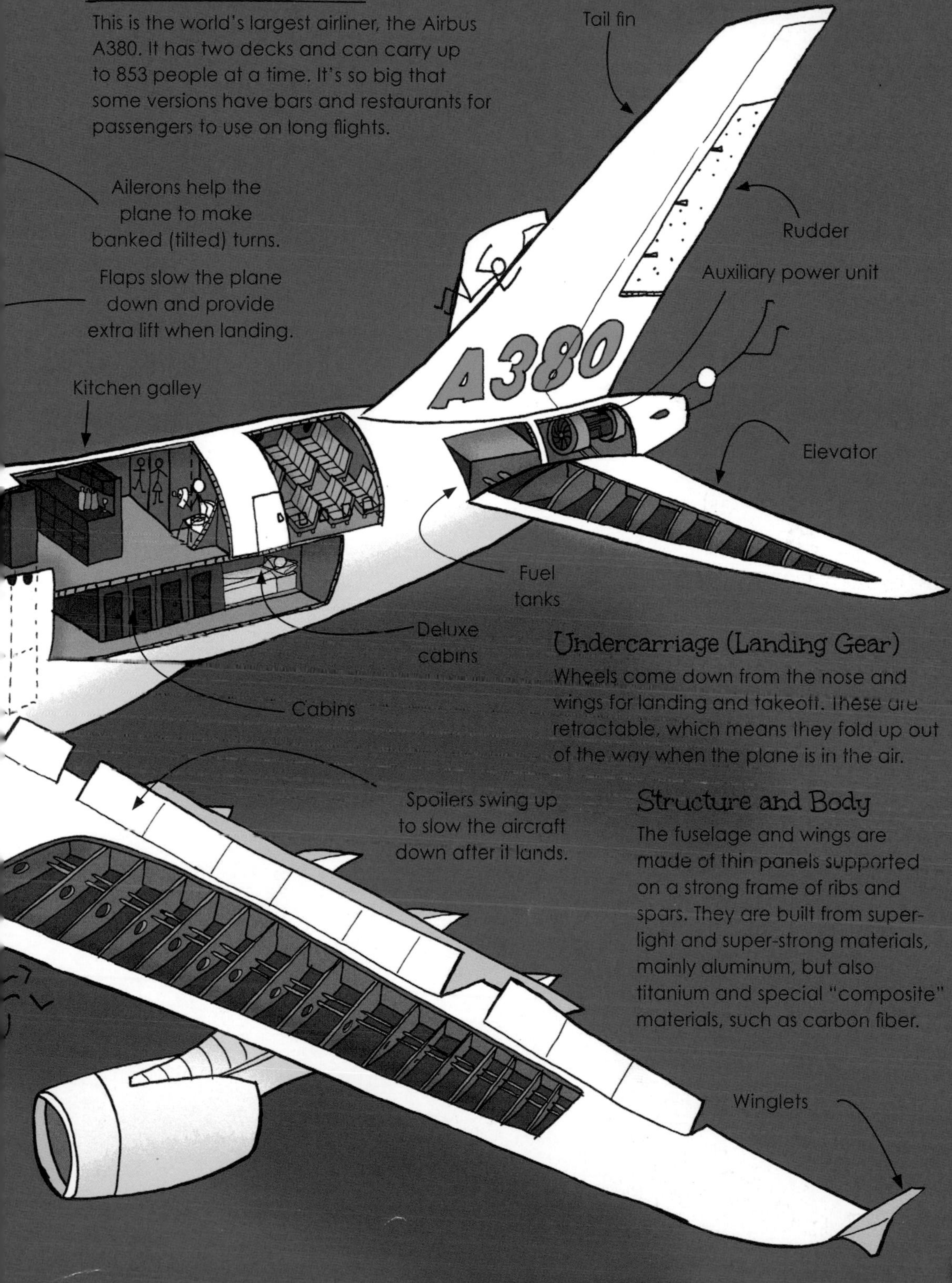

Ailerons help the plane to make banked (tilted) turns.

Flaps slow the plane down and provide extra lift when landing.

Tail fin

Rudder

Auxiliary power unit

Kitchen galley

Elevator

Fuel tanks

Deluxe cabins

Cabins

Undercarriage (Landing Gear)

Wheels come down from the nose and wings for landing and takeoff. These are retractable, which means they fold up out of the way when the plane is in the air.

Spoilers swing up to slow the aircraft down after it lands.

Structure and Body

The fuselage and wings are made of thin panels supported on a strong frame of ribs and spars. They are built from super-light and super-strong materials, mainly aluminum, but also titanium and special "composite" materials, such as carbon fiber.

Winglets

Wings

While a plane is moving fast enough, its wings provide the lift that keeps it airborne. As wings slice through the air (right), air is forced up and over them. The air stretches out and drops in pressure, so the wings are pushed up by the higher air pressure beneath. The pilot controls the plane by moving flaps on the wing edges to vary the lift that each wing provides.

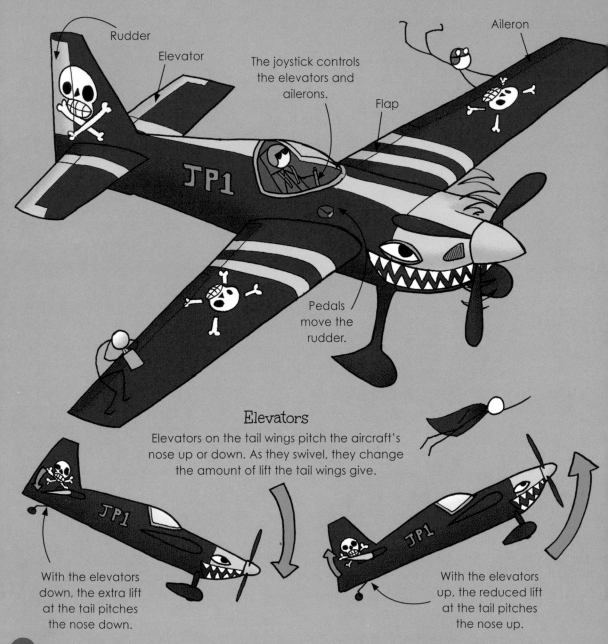

Rudder

Elevator

Aileron

The joystick controls the elevators and ailerons.

Flap

JP1

Pedals move the rudder.

Elevators

Elevators on the tail wings pitch the aircraft's nose up or down. As they swivel, they change the amount of lift the tail wings give.

With the elevators down, the extra lift at the tail pitches the nose down.

With the elevators up, the reduced lift at the tail pitches the nose up.

The Shape of Wings

Wings work because they have a special curved shape, or camber, and cut through the air at a slight angle called the angle of attack. This is what forces the air up and over to create lift. Up to a point, the greater the camber and angle of attack, the greater the lift.

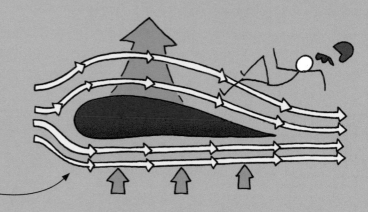

Ailerons

Ailerons make the plane roll to left or right by lifting one wing more than the other. In combination with the rudder, they enable the plane to bank and turn.

Left aileron up, right aileron down makes the plane roll to the left.

Left aileron down, right aileron up makes the plane roll to the right.

Rudder

The rudder is the upright flap on the tail. Swinging it to the left makes the plane steer or "yaw" left. Swinging it to the right makes it steer right.

Flaps

Lowering the flaps helps the plane to land. It slows the plane down by increasing drag and generates the extra lift needed to keep the plane in the air at slow speeds.

Flight Controls

There is no road to guide you up in the air, so pilots rely on instruments to tell them where they are and which way to go. In modern airliners, the instruments are linked to the plane's control systems and fly the plane automatically most of the time.

Six-Pack

All planes still have six basic instruments. These are now mostly backups in case the electronic display fails.

1 The airspeed indicator shows how fast the plane is flying in knots. A knot is just a little more than 1 mph.

2 The attitude indicator or artificial horizon shows how level the plane is flying—for example, if it is banked to one side or pitched to nose or tail.

3 The altimeter shows how far above the ground the plane is flying, in feet.

4 The turn indicator shows how fast and steeply the plane is banking on a turn.

5 The heading indicator is a compass. It shows the pilot which direction the plane is heading and allows the plane to fly on a chosen compass bearing.

6. The vertical speed indicator shows how fast the plane is climbing or descending.

Fly-by-Wire

In old planes, the pilot's controls moved the wing flaps through rods and levers. Modern planes are "fly-by-wire": electric wires control motors that move the flaps.

In manual flight, the pilot's controls operate a computer that sends wire signals to move the flaps.

In autopilot, the plane's flight control computer takes over from the pilot, making adjustments to the flight automatically in response to data from the instruments.

Captain's Seat

The flight captain sits in the left-hand seat and the copilot in the right-hand seat of the cockpit. The copilot has exactly the same controls as the captain.

Primary flight display
All the basic instruments, including the artificial horizon and airspeed indicator, are combined in a single electronic screen display.

Autopilot
The pilot usually controls the plane manually for takeoff and landing, and switches on the autopilot once the plane is at cruising height.

Sidestick
In manual flight, the pilot controls the flaps using the handle at their side, called a sidestick.

Navigation display
The navigation display feeds information from satellites, radio beacons, and radar to an electronic map showing everything the pilot needs to know.

Engine display
This gives a continual update on how the engines are performing.

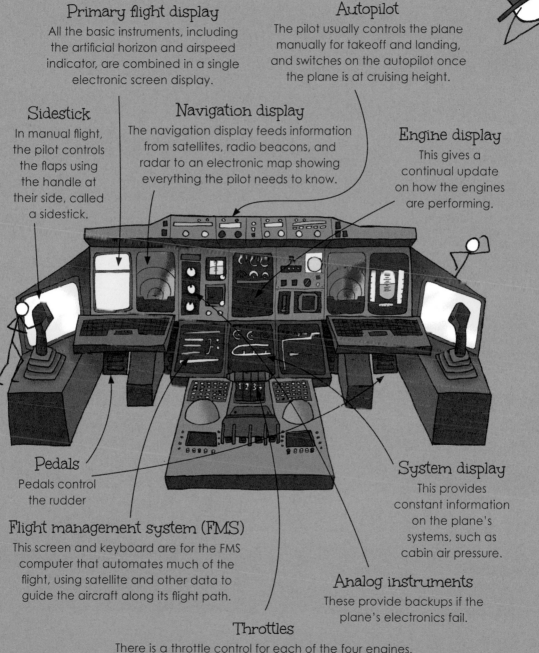

Pedals
Pedals control the rudder

System display
This provides constant information on the plane's systems, such as cabin air pressure.

Flight management system (FMS)
This screen and keyboard are for the FMS computer that automates much of the flight, using satellite and other data to guide the aircraft along its flight path.

Analog instruments
These provide backups if the plane's electronics fail.

Throttles
There is a throttle control for each of the four engines. Pushing the lever forward increases the power.

Jet Engines

Like cars, planes used to have engines with heavy pistons that clank up and down. Most bigger planes now have jet engines. These engines have only fans that whiz around inside a tube, gulping in huge quantities of air. They are very powerful and light, but they are noisy and only work well at high speeds.

Turboprop

Many smaller airplanes and cargo planes have turboprop engines. These are jet engines that turn a propeller and work better at lower speeds than a turbofan jet engine.

1   Air is drawn into the front of the engine by a fan.

2   The air is mixed with fuel and ignited in the combustion chamber.

3   The burning fuel and air expand and push against a kind of fan called a turbine, spinning it around.

4   As the turbine spins, it turns the driveshaft and a gearbox.

5   The gearbox sets the propeller spinning.

6   The propeller spins.

7   The propeller pulls the plane along.

Cutting Edge

The propeller blades on turboprops are usually curved back like a scimitar sword. Like swept-back wings, the curve stops them from dragging so much as they cut very fast through the air.

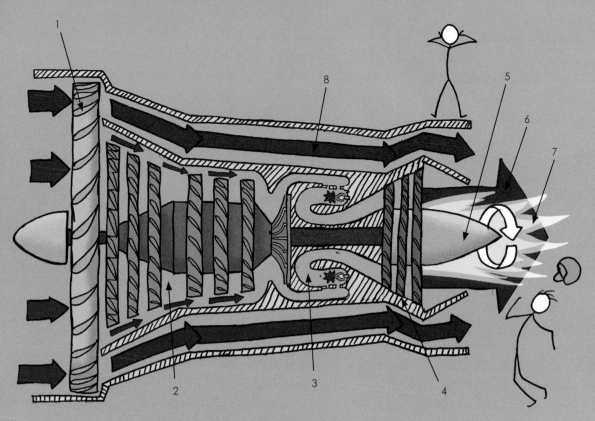

Turbofan

Most modern airliners use a variation on the basic jet engine called a turbofan. This has a second large fan at the front to draw in an extra flow of air that bypasses the engine core where the fuel and air burn. This makes the engine run more quietly at takeoff speeds.

1   A large fan sucks in air at the front.
2   Some of the air is blown into the compressor fan.
3   The compressor fan squeezes the air into the combustion chamber, where it is mixed with jet fuel and set alight.
4   The burning fuel expands rapidly and rushes past each turbine's blades, spinning them like a windmill.
5   The spinning turbine spins the compressor fan.
6   The hot gases roar out very fast from the back of the engine as a hot jet.

7   As the jet shoots backward out of the engine, it thrusts the plane forward.
8   The bypass air is blown around the outside of the combustion chamber and straight out of the back.

Massive Fan

Turbofans are easily identified by the giant fan in the front of the engine.

Alternative Power

Jets are very noisy, and the fuel they burn is expensive and causes pollution. So aircraft designers are experimenting with electric, solar, and even pedal power as alternative ways of powering planes. These experiments include the Solar Impulse project, with its two operational solar-powered aircraft.

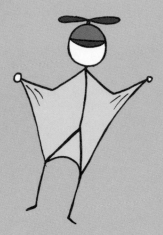

Sun Power

Solar planes have huge panels of solar cells on the wings. These convert sunlight into electricity to power electric motors. On the solar plane Solar Impulse 2, the solar panels also charge up a bank of lithium batteries during the day so the plane can fly at night.

Solar Impulse 2

Solar Impulse 2 is the most ambitious solar-powered plane yet. It can fly long distances by combining chargeable batteries with solar power. In 2015, it began an attempt to fly around the world by flying five days and five nights nonstop across the Pacific Ocean.

Wings are covered in 17,000 solar cells.

Cockpit

As Solar Impulse 2 flies around the world, the pilot will have to sit alone in the cockpit for five or six days at a time. The tiny cockpit has no air conditioning, so can get very hot or very cold. There is a parachute and a life raft if things go wrong…

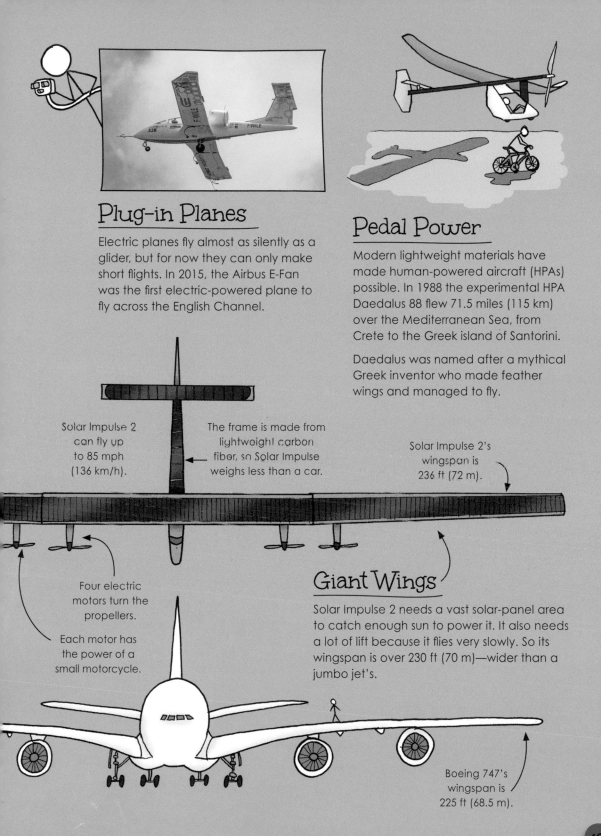

Plug-in Planes

Electric planes fly almost as silently as a glider, but for now they can only make short flights. In 2015, the Airbus E-Fan was the first electric-powered plane to fly across the English Channel.

Pedal Power

Modern lightweight materials have made human-powered aircraft (HPAs) possible. In 1988 the experimental HPA Daedalus 88 flew 71.5 miles (115 km) over the Mediterranean Sea, from Crete to the Greek island of Santorini.

Daedalus was named after a mythical Greek inventor who made feather wings and managed to fly.

Solar Impulse 2 can fly up to 85 mph (136 km/h).

The frame is made from lightweight carbon fiber, so Solar Impulse weighs less than a car.

Solar Impulse 2's wingspan is 236 ft (72 m).

Four electric motors turn the propellers.

Each motor has the power of a small motorcycle.

Giant Wings

Solar Impulse 2 needs a vast solar-panel area to catch enough sun to power it. It also needs a lot of lift because it flies very slowly. So its wingspan is over 230 ft (70 m)—wider than a jumbo jet's.

Boeing 747's wingspan is 225 ft (68.5 m).

Vertical Takeoff

Most ordinary planes need a long runway to build up the speed to lift off. Vertical takeoff and landing (VTOL) planes have the same fixed wings, but also special engines that can power them straight up into the air for takeoff and lower them gently for landing.

Straight-up Fighter

The Lockheed Martin F35 Lightning II may be the most versatile fighter plane ever. Not only can it fly at supersonic speeds, up to 1,200 mph (1,930 km/h), it can also take off and land vertically and hover in midair like a helicopter.

Control flaps

Swivel Power

In level flight, the jet thrust from the F35's mighty Rolls-Royce jet engine roars straight out at the back and powers it to supersonic speeds. But the exhaust nozzle can swivel to direct the hot jet downward for takeoff.

The swiveling exhaust nozzle is known as a 3-bearing swivel module, or 3BSM, and blasts out 43,000 lb of thrust.

Twin tail fins

Up and Down

To take off vertically, or in a short space, the F35 opens the lift fan doors and turns the swivel jet to point down. At once, a surge of cool air from the lift fan and hot air from the swivel jet thrusts the plane upwards. The plane rises powerfully into the air, kept in balance by the roll posts.

To hover, the F35 keeps the downthrust from the lift fan in balance with the weight of the plane.

To land, the F35 reverses the takeoff procedure, gradually reducing power to lower the plane.

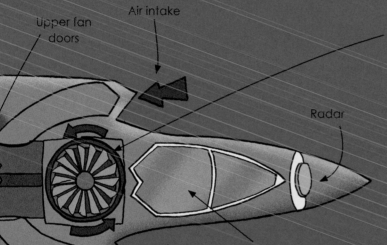

Upper fan doors

Air intake

Radar

Cockpit

Missile bay

Landing gear in wheel bay, which can be used for both vertical and horizontal takeoff

Roll posts

To steady the plane when taking off and hovering, the pilot can fire the jet thrusters in each wing. These get their power through ducts from the main engine called roll posts. Each delivers about 1,000 lb of thrust.

Lift fan

Just behind the cockpit is the lift fan. This super-powerful fan is mounted horizontally and driven by a shaft from the engine. There are two fans rotating in opposite directions and blowing out cool air.

Upthrust

In level flight, the lift fan is hidden under folding doors. But for vertical takeoff, the doors open. Air is then sucked in through the top of the fan and blasted out through the bottom to create an upthrust of over 40,000 lb that powers the plane straight up.

Helicopters

Ordinary aircraft must fly forward nonstop for the wings to lift them. But a helicopter's wings are rotor blades that give lift simply by spinning around and around. That's why helicopters can take off and land almost vertically and hover in midair.

The Tail Rotor

One potential problem is that the helicopter itself, rather than the rotor blades, might spin around. This is solved by a small vertical tail rotor that pulls the helicopter around in the opposite direction to the rotors.

Tail boom

Tail rotor

Forward, Backward, and Sideways

Normally, the rotor pulls the helicopter straight up. But the pilot can tilt the blades to increase or reduce the pitch at a particular point as they go around. This is called cyclic pitch control and angles the blades ahead, behind, left, or right, so the helicopter can fly in that direction.

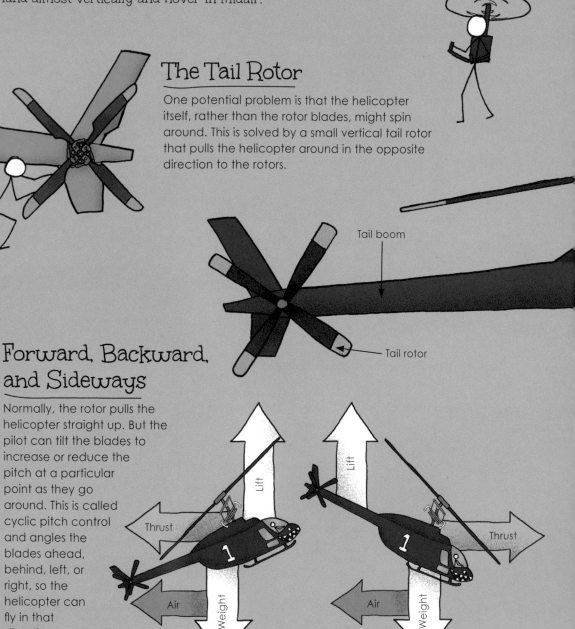

Lift

Thrust

Air

Weight

Lift

Thrust

Air

Weight

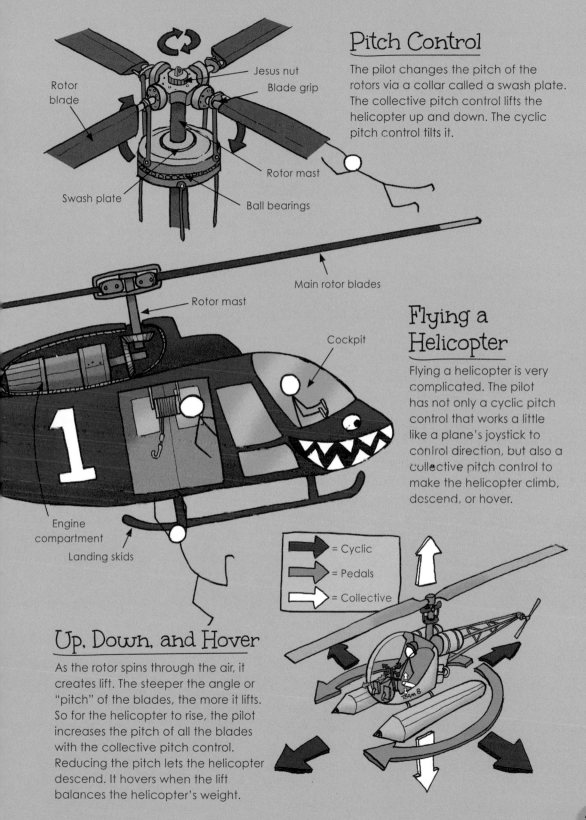

Pitch Control

The pilot changes the pitch of the rotors via a collar called a swash plate. The collective pitch control lifts the helicopter up and down. The cyclic pitch control tilts it.

Rotor blade

Jesus nut

Blade grip

Rotor mast

Swash plate

Ball bearings

Main rotor blades

Rotor mast

Cockpit

Flying a Helicopter

Flying a helicopter is very complicated. The pilot has not only a cyclic pitch control that works a little like a plane's joystick to control direction, but also a collective pitch control to make the helicopter climb, descend, or hover.

Engine compartment

Landing skids

= Cyclic

= Pedals

= Collective

Up, Down, and Hover

As the rotor spins through the air, it creates lift. The steeper the angle or "pitch" of the blades, the more it lifts. So for the helicopter to rise, the pilot increases the pitch of all the blades with the collective pitch control. Reducing the pitch lets the helicopter descend. It hovers when the lift balances the helicopter's weight.

Balloons and Airships

You don't always need wings to fly. Balloons and airships float up into the air using gases lighter than air. Some balloons are bags filled with hot air or light helium gas to make them rise. Airships are lifted by a long, semi-rigid envelope filled with helium. You can't steer a hot-air balloon, which goes where the wind blows it. But you can fly in the direction you want if you pick the right wind conditions.

As the burner heats the air it becomes less dense and rises. The hot air then shapes the balloon. The hot air is lighter and less dense than the air outside, so it floats away and carries the balloon with it.

Making Hot Air

The burners are the balloon's engines. They burn propane gas to fill the balloon with hot air and make it rise. To stay aloft, the pilot keeps adding more hot air. To descend, the air is allowed to cool or let out through the top of the balloon.

Passengers and crew are carried in a light basket suspended beneath the balloon.

Airship

The difference between a balloon and an airship is not just the shape. An airship has engines, which means it can be flown in whatever direction you want. A century ago, vast airships carried passengers in luxury across the Atlantic.

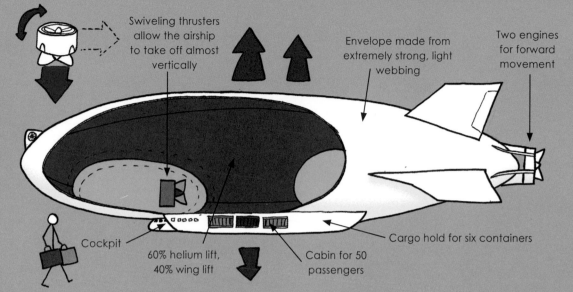

Swiveling thrusters allow the airship to take off almost vertically

Envelope made from extremely strong, light webbing

Two engines for forward movement

Cockpit

60% helium lift, 40% wing lift

Cabin for 50 passengers

Cargo hold for six containers

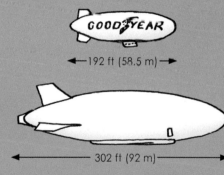

←—192 ft (58.5 m)—→

←———— 302 ft (92 m) ————→

Airlander 10

The experimental Airlander 10 is an airship being built in the UK. When it is complete, it will be by far the largest aircraft in the world: 302 ft (92 m) long, 143 ft (43.5 m) wide, and 85 ft (26 m) tall. But that is small compared to the giant airship planned for the future, which the makers hope can help in survey work and disaster relief.

Not all of the Airlander's lift comes from the lighter-than-air helium gas that fills its envelope. When full, it is shaped like a wing, and as the propellers drive it forward, the shape provides lift, too.

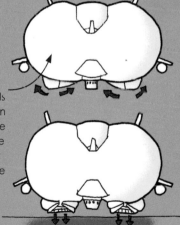

Landing Cushion

The Airlander has no landing wheels. Instead it shoots out its own inflatable cushion for landing, along with jets of air. That means it can land anywhere, even on water.

Drones

You don't need a pilot to fly a plane. Drones, or "unmanned aerial vehicles" (UAVs), are robot aircraft that can fly by themselves. Some don't even need a controller on the ground to send them instructions, but are controlled by electronic programs instead.

Flying Eyes

Drones give a great bird's-eye view of inaccessible places, or places too dangerous for people to go. Many are basically flying cameras, used by police to track criminals, aid agencies to monitor disasters in dangerous conditions, and even film crews to shoot thrilling overhead views.

Military drones are packed with sensors, including video and still cameras, image intensifiers, thermal imagers, and laser rangefinders.

Remote Control

Large, sophisticated drones, like those used by the military, need a crew of three on the ground: a pilot and two sensor operators. To fly the drone, the pilot moves a joystick just as if flying a real plane, but has to rely on a narrow camera view. If the drone is out of view, the signals are relayed to the drone via a satellite.

Quadcopters

While large military drones are more like ordinary planes with wings, most smaller drones are special kinds of helicopters called quadcopters. Quadcopters have not just one rotor but four.

In the future, you might receive deliveries wherever you are by drones that home in on your smartphone.

The quadcopter changes direction and height by varying the relative speed of the rotors.

Unlike on ordinary helicopters, the pitch of the rotors on a quadcopter is fixed.

The speed of the four rotors is electronically coordinated.

Moving the control to the left increases the rotation of the right-hand rotors, so the quadcopter banks left.

A camera lets filmmakers use drones for aerial views.

Moving the control to the right increases the rotation of the left-hand rotors, so the quadcopter banks right.

If the quadcopter is out of sight, it can be controlled with the aid of a virtual reality headset, which continually feeds the view seen by the drone's cameras.

Quadcopters for businesses, emergencies, and home use are operated by devices rather like video game controllers. You can control some of the simplest quadcopters with just a

Rockets

Getting things into space demands a huge amount of power—the kind of power only rockets can provide. Unlike jet and piston engines, rocket engines have few moving parts. They rely entirely on the massive force of expansion of burning rocket fuel.

Launch Stages

Most of a rocket's weight is fuel, and it uses most of it simply getting off the ground. So rather than carrying vast tanks with them for an entire journey, spacecraft are built in parts. After they are launched, rockets used for launching are jettisoned in stages.

3 Less than four minutes after launch and 100 miles (160 km) up, the main rockets have burned all their fuel and cut out. They too are jettisoned, and the second-stage rockets, a smaller version of the main rockets, fire up.

Payload

The payload is whatever the rocket is launching into space. It could be a satellite destined to orbit the earth, or a space probe on a mission to distant planets. Or it could be a module carrying astronauts to a space station or even further.

Fuel

Oxygen

Pumps and valves

Combustion chamber

2 Two minutes after launch and over 30 miles (48 km) up, the solid boosters cut out and fall away. The main rockets, powered by liquid fuel—liquid oxygen and hydrogen—fire to blast the spacecraft up to over 10,000 mph (16,000 km/h).

1 To give the kick it needs to take off from the launch pad, the spacecraft has solid rocket boosters strapped to its side. They use gunpowder-like solid fuel that burns ferociously but briefly.

A rocket is propelled by the reaction between the expanding gases and the body of the rocket.

4 The fairing (protective covering) for the payload falls away, and after six minutes the second-stage rockets also burn out and fall away, leaving the payload to continue by itself.

Rocket for Deep Space

It will take a hugely powerful rocket to launch a spacecraft big enough to carry astronauts as far as Mars. So NASA are developing their Space Launch System. It will be the most powerful rocket ever built, with five engines in its main stage.

At the top of the Space Launch System (SLS) is the Multi-Purpose Crew Vehicle in which astronauts will travel to the moon or Mars. It consists of four parts:

Launch abort: an escape capsule for the crew in case anything goes wrong early in the flight

Crew module: the small, conical compartment in which the astronauts travel. It's so tiny that the four-person crew has little room to move around.

Service module: contains the engines, the solar panels that collect energy, and the crew's oxygen generator

Adapter: attaches the module to the booster

Rocket Sizes

The biggest and most powerful rockets yet were the Saturn V rockets that launched the Apollo missions carrying astronauts to the moon between 1968 and 1972. Each was 363 ft (110 m) tall and blasted a payload of 260,000 lb (117,900 kg)—as much as 20 buses—up into space.

Strange Inventions

Wacky designs for flying machines from the last century (and before)...

The Plane for Rain?

Who said an aircraft has to have two long wings? New York inventor William Romme didn't think so. With the help of Chance Vought he built the Cycloplane in Chicago. It came to be called the Umbrella Plane because its fabric wings were stretched over spokes just like an umbrella. Amazingly, it actually flew a number of times between 1911 and 1913.

In a Flap

Countless inventors have been inspired by the birds to build aircraft with flapping wings. Aircraft like this are called ornithopters. The first was designed by the 15th-century Italian genius Leonardo da Vinci. One of the more successful was George White's pedal-powered ornithopter, which flew almost a mile along St. Augustine Beach in Florida in 1928. People are still trying to build ornithopters even now.

Flying Saucer

Who said flying saucers come from outer space? In the 1950s, the US military and Avro Canada teamed up to build one in secret. They named it the Avrocar, though some called it the Silver Bug. It lifted off using the downdraft from a powerful turbofan in the middle. It only flew at 35 mph (56 km/h) and hovered just a few feet off the ground. But Avro engineers thought it might fly at 300 mph (480 km/h) and reach 10,000 ft (3,048 m).

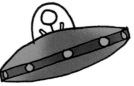

Sea Skimmer

Russian engineer Rostislav Alexeyev realized there was no need for planes to fly high. If they flew just above the surface of the earth, they experienced a bonus lift known as the ground effect. In the 1980s, his team developed the Lun-class Ekranoplan Ground Effect Vehicle. This was a giant seaplane more than 200 ft (60 m) long that skimmed just 12 ft (3.6 m) above the surface of the sea and yet remained undetected by radar.

Wing Ding Ring

The earliest planes had not just one pair of wings, but often two (biplanes) or even three (triplanes). In 1907, a French navy engineer, the Marquis d'Equevilly, built his Multiplane, with five pairs of half wings and two full wings, all enclosed in a pair of hoops. The next year he built another version with 50 wings!

Glossary

Aileron

Hinged flap on the outside edge of the wing that allows the plane to roll to one side or the other

Airfoil

Special shape of an aircraft wing, with a curved surface that provides lift

Altimeter

Instrument that tells the pilot how high the plane is flying

Autopilot

System for controlling the aircraft automatically, without the pilot's input

Bank

Airplane turn in which the plane tilts at an angle as it turns

Cockpit

The place where the pilot and copilot sit

Collective pitch

The angle of all the rotor blades of a helicopter

Cyclic pitch

When the rotor blades of a helicopter change pitch at a particular part of their rotation

Elevator

Hinged flap on the rear wings that controls the pitch of an aircraft

Flap

Hinged surface on the outside edge of the wing that controls the lift and speed of the plane

Fuselage

The central body of an aircraft

Joystick

The handle that the pilot uses to control the plane by moving wing flaps

Pitch

The tilt of the plane from back to front

Solar cell

Unit that converts sunlight to electricity, also known as a photo-voltaic cell

Turbofan

Jet engine that runs more quietly by using an extra fan to provide a bypass of cool air

Turboprop

Jet engine that uses the jet thrust to turn a propeller

Yaw

When the plane steers one way or the other without banking

INDEX

The Author

John Farndon is Royal Literary Fellow at Anglia Ruskin University in Cambridge, UK. He has written numerous books for adults and children on science, technology, and nature, and been shortlisted four times for the Royal Society's Young People's Book Prize. He has recently created science stories for children for the Moscow Polytech science festival.

The Illustrator

John Paul de Quay has a BSc in Biology from the University of Sussex, UK, and a graduate certificate in animation from the University of the West of England. He devotes his spare time to growing chilli peppers, perfecting his plan for a sustainable future, and caring for a small plastic dinosaur. He has three pet squid that live in the bath, which makes drawing in ink quite economical…

Picture Credits (abbreviations: t = top; b = bottom; c = center; l = left; r = right)
© www.shutterstock.com: 6 cr, 6 bl, 7 tr, 7 br, 8 tl, 8 cc, 8 cr, 9 tl, 9 tr, 9 bl, 9 br, 17 br

7 cl Alberto Loyo / Shutterstock.com, 8 tr EtiAmmos / Shutterstock.com, 8 bl Lefteris Papaulakis / Shutterstock.com, 9 tbr John Kropewnicki / Shutterstock.com, 9 cr AlexanderZam / Shutterstock.com, 9 cl Paul Drabot / Shutterstock. com, 16 br Bocman1973 / Shutterstock.com , 19 tl De Visu / Shutterstock.com, 26 bc thomas koch / Shutterstock.com